Helping Big Cats

by Isabel Thomas
Illustrated by Jean Claude

Contents

OXFORD

UNIVERSITY PRESS

What Are Big Cats?

Big cats are the world's largest cats. Pet cats are tiny compared to them!

Lions, tigers, leopards, cheetahs, jaguars and lynx are all types of big cats.

Many big cats have coats with <u>patterns</u>. We can tell what type of big cat it is by the <u>pattern</u>.

ears

tail

longer hair

spots

brown fur

Can you see a coat with a stripy <u>pattern</u>?
What other <u>patterns</u> can you see?

Why Do Big Cats Need Help?

Big cats are powerful predators. They hunt other animals for food, even huge animals like buffaloes and giraffes! However, many of these powerful predators are in danger of dying out because of humans.

The numbers of big cats go down year on year. They all need help now.

Humans have spoilt the places where big cats live. We have changed forests and grasslands into farms. We have built huge towns and cities. In some places, big cats only have a <u>tiny</u> space left to live in.

Why do you think big cats need a big space rather than a <u>tiny</u> space to live?

Farmers need land for farms but big cats need land too. The cats need lots of room to hunt for food.

Why Do People Harm Big Cats?

Sometimes people hunt big cats for sport or for the beautiful patterns on their coats. It is hard to <u>understand</u> why anybody would do this.

Sometimes people attack big cats because they are afraid that the big cats will harm them or their farm animals.

It is hard living near big cats if you fear them.

Do you <u>understand</u> why some people are afraid of big cats?

Who Helps Big Cats?

Lots of animal experts help big cats. They also <u>promise</u> to help local people live safely near big cats. For example, experts show farmers how to build special fences around their farms. It is hard for big cats to find the <u>entrance</u> in these special fences.

Look at the picture of the farm. It is hard for big cats to find the <u>entrance</u> in the fence. How does this help the farmer?

If farmers feel secure, they will not kill big cats.

Farmers <u>promise</u> not to harm lions if their cattle are protected. What <u>promises</u> could you make to help animals?

Scientists are helping big cats too. They try to understand how big cats live so we can find new ways to protect them.
Scientists are <u>careful</u> not to disturb the big cats. Instead of getting close to them, scientists study clues that big cats leave behind.

If you are <u>careful</u>, you do things safely to make sure you do not get hurt. What else might the scientists do to be <u>careful</u>?

What Is Next For Big Cats?

Lots of people, like scientists and conservation workers, are trying to help big cats. It is important that as many people as possible understand that big cats are still endangered.

We can tell adults that big cats need help.

Think About the Book

What is happening in each picture? Can you remember some ways people are helping big cats?